FOOTPATH GU

AROUND REIGATE AND REDHILL

REIGATE PRIORY LAKE

CONTENTS

CONTENTS

LIST OF ILLUSTRATIONS

FOREWORD

IT is generally accepted that Surrey contains as much fine scenery as any found in the Home Counties, and in the south-eastern corner can be found as much variety as in any other parts of the county. Again, the adjacent counties of Sussex and Kent are so close that we go over their borders in some of these walks.

There is no better way of seeing the real country in all its intimacy than by walking the paths made and used by country folk before the roads were there. To understand the domestic habits of the birds, to see the animals in the fields and the lovely little cottages with their trim gardens, it is best to get away from the roads and go along paths that in some places are almost forgotten.

The exercise of walking is so beneficial that it is worth much on that account alone, while the memories of a walk amid pleasant scenery will enable you to pluck chords of remembrance whenever a dull moment occurs, and you can go over the whole way again in retrospect, especially if you have the book at hand.

A walk can be enjoyed three times over: the preparation, when you read about it and view the prospect in your mind; the actual walk, which may be even finer than you visualised ; and afterwards, perhaps in a comfortable chair, you will have the pleasure of thinking about it and enjoying it again in your mind.

INTRODUCTION

LET me make one point clear at the start: the Borough of Reigate embraces all that is called Reigate or Redhill. When Reigate was old enough to have a history, Red Hill was only a hill, so called because of the colour of its trees or soil, and it is only the railway that has made it of any importance. Many people think of them as being distinct towns, yet Redhill may be taken as the commercial side of Reigate. Even the Brighton roads have been divided, one running through Croydon to Redhill, while the other takes Sutton in its stride and crosses through Reigate by Reigate Hill. They meet at Povey Cross, just below Horley, whence, after a couple of miles, Sussex is entered just beyond Lowfield Heath.

In these walks we touch at many points on the two Brighton roads, but we also go along a much older road—The Pilgrim's Way. This old road from Winchester to Canterbury can be traced in parts, often bordered by hedges of ancient yews, and mostly lying on the dry and sunny side of the Downs. It was the route of the pilgrimage by those doing penance and finally gathering at St. Thomas à Becket's grave. Traces of the way may be found in the name of one road by which

Reigate is entered: Slipshoe Street. Apparently the pilgrims shed their muddy footwear here before donning their town attire. The white scoring of the path called The Pilgrim's Way along the edge of Colley Hill is visible from many points as we pass, and will give direction when viewed from a vantage-point.

Naturally, the range of hills which includes Colley, Reigate and White Hills are the immediate scenes with which we are keen to gain intimacy.

There are other items of interest which will not escape those who have them as part of their particular aim in these walks. The Surrey churches within this area are quite as interesting as those in other parts of the country.

If you are an antiquarian, or only a lover of old houses, you will find the walk through Brewer Street will give you a lot of pleasure. There are many more which are mentioned, and probably others which have been omitted. Of inns, there are the usual Surrey ones, which means good fare, if of a homely type. Many of them are passed on these walks.

Botanists may find on the hills many a rare flower that grows in the chalk, and as sand and clay prevail in other places, the vasculum will be well filled with specimens on your return. Orchids—even the rare ones—have been gathered by those who know their habits, but no naturalist gives away the actual secret source of his prize.

Some birds love the hills, others the valleys or towns, but the majority of common birds love the hills near a town. The B.B.C. has recorded bird songs at Leigh—or near there ; and many visitors come to the area for bird-watching. It is, therefore, a district which will give you plenty of opportunity for ornithological study. If by chance you would like to hear the nightingale, your wish may be easily gratified. Along the Brighton road, by Earlswood Common and Maple Woods, there are always trills to be heard of that sweetest of songsters directly after twilight in the spring, no matter how heavy the traffic in the main road. Near Salfords station, about the end of April, every year, I have heard the nightingale singing its heart out, even when air raids were in progress.

Helix Pomatia, a large edible snail, may be found on many parts of Reigate Hill. It is said to have been introduced by French pilgrims, but other theories have been put forward.

Place-names are of interest to antiquarians. Brockham is derived from Brocksholm—the haunt of the badger ; Tilgate, Faygate, Newdigate (entrances) ; Hartswood, Hookwood, Charlwood, Kingswood and Earlswood must all be derived from the times when the great forest of Anderida spread over the area, before the timber had been used for iron-smelting. The ironstone was smelted with charcoal made from the forest trees. Woodhatch, the gate into the wood, was in later years the place where the turnpike gate stood. A ley, being a clearing or pasture-land, may be traced in Horley or Crawley. Merstham was Merstan, which can be read as Mere-stan, the stone by the lake.

As regards the best time of year to walk along these paths, I have made a point of walking in the district all the year round. There is something different to see each season. There are parts of the district which are best left to the drier times of the year, particularly where the river Mole derives its life blood. The Leigh-Newdigate corner can be very damp in winter, and footpaths between Outwood, Salfords and Horley are not attractive in wet weather. Take these when they are dry ; they are delightful and well away from the track of the usual footpath walker. The village of Charlwood and nearby Glovers Wood are worth an extra exploration ; they may be reached by 'bus from Horley, and a very interesting half-day spent there. There is still a good path leading from the church, directly through to Newdigate Place, with its deer and ponds, although the deer have been non-existent, as far as the walker is concerned, since the military occupied part of it.

The walker may find notices in his wanderings that seem to be especially aimed at him. At the side of many paths are warnings that 'Trespassers will be prosecuted.' This usually applies to the land on each side of the right-of-way, and the owner may perhaps hope that it will warn you off the path, too. During the war, there were many notices of a pertinent type, which we always respected. While the paths given here are all rights-of-way, as far as we know, if any walker is pulled up he should remember to be as tactful as possible, as he may have inadvertently strayed off the actual path, and offer to pay for damage should he have caused any. Incidentally, you should not be ordered to go back to where you came in, but should have the opportunity of regaining the route at the nearest point. This is the footpath law. The following routes, even for short walks, will show you Nature at her best, and with the intimacy that can only be had by getting away from main roads and walking into the country along footpaths.

Good luck and good walking !

I. OVER THE DOWNS

Redhill, Reigate Hill, Colley Hill, Walton Heath, Headley, Happy Valley, Boxhill, Stepping Stones, Brockham Green, Betchworth, Reigate Heath.

ALMOST the first thing that strikes the visitor to Reigate or Redhill is the dominating sight of the Downs. They stand as a background and an invitation. Let us, then, make their acquaintance on our first walk.

From Redhill station, or the Green Line coach-stop, go along the Reigate road to Warwick Hotel, turn right up Warwick road for a few yards towards two posts, which start our path, on the left. This path goes behind St. Matthew's church. At the road, bear left for a few yards, and again right up Batts Hill. Just beyond the nursing home (left) a gate leads to an uphill path, which ends in a road where we bear left.

On approaching Wray Common you will see a fine windmill, backed by Gatton Park. Seen with its cluster of houses on a windy day it is quite an imposing picture—though only ornamental now. Cross over to Wray Lane and continue. Just after a road-sign and by a pillar-box turn down a left incline and, keeping left, you will enter a valley, an amphitheatre crowned with bushes.

This is a delightful picnicking spot, and very few of the hundreds of people who sit on top of Reigate Hill know of it. Listening, you may hear many kinds of birds, and even a woodpecker tapping in the copse, but you will seldom meet other people. When you have made a semi-circle, look for a path on the right, crossing over another and going uphill. It becomes very steep, and on reaching the top turn right to a path edged by rails. There is a good view over these railings towards the South Downs.

Turn up the steps on the left and on to where seats have been placed. You will see Chanctonbury Ring, and Reigate Park may be picked out if you know its contours. To the right of the refreshment hut, an incline leads to the suspension bridge, and this is where walkers from Reigate would join the path, coming from Reigate station up the hill. Over the bridge, keep on through the avenue of trees. Follow the sign-post to Queen's Park. About 100 yards beyond the water-tower, a break in the hedge shows the famous beeches. There is not much of a path through them, but keep parallel with the path you have been on ; it improves, and finishes at a water-fountain.

Cobbett said of this glorious view that it

COLLEY HILL

was the finest in the world. In the distance can be picked out Leith Hill, Betchworth Clump, and the whole sweep of the Downs, starting with the slopes of Colley Hill. But the best of the walk is yet to come. Keep to the crest of the hill, dodging the big holes by going round, but just beyond the water-tower keep forward and do not continue further round the crest. You should come to another path by a house and green posts. If out for only a morning's walk turn left at a gravel path, and on coming to a cottage and three gates take a path by a 'Private' sign (this refers to the drive). This path then carries on for a mile, becoming first a track and then a road, and will lead to Reigate Heath near the Black Horse, where a 'bus service operates.

To continue the full walk, keep on past the green posts, going by part of Walton Heath golf-course, until arriving at the bend and a notice with two paths on the left. Go along one which says 'No Horses' to a cluster of houses and a wall. When the road branches right, go by a path over the heath between the two roads. It may be overgrown, but it comes out about a mile above Pebble Hill, and on the other side of the road is a path to Headley (sign). Where the path is swampy, as it sometimes is, get up on the field above and keep along the hedge ; approach the back of a house (the original path joins just before) and look for gate (half-left) ; turn left when over it and go round a wall past a farmhouse. Bear right where the track goes round ; in about half a mile it enters a plantation and, just beyond, watch for a stile by the side of a gate. There is not much of a path to guide you, but keep along a wooden fence to a stile under some trees. Turn left from the stile over which you see a red farm.

This is a good place from which to contemplate the countryside. How convenient these gates are ! A few yards further on, a sign-post directs you to Headley ; we carry on up the road, right, looking for the spire of Headley church. We would have seen Kingswood church when coming by Walton Heath, and we may have got a glimpse of Ranmore on the way, too.

The village is a mecca for walkers, and there is refreshment there also. At the Cock Inn they sell beer by the pound, according to the notice. We presume it means by the sheep-pound.

On the opposite side of the road a footpath goes to Mickleham (sign-post), a delightful little path, going by a bombed house on the left, crossing the road (keeping left for a few yards and almost opposite a pretty cottage) on to another road sign-posted to Mickleham. Keep along this for about a mile and a half.

This district has been named Little Switzerland, and that gives an idea of its beauty. You may get a glimpse of Ranmore church spire on your way ; it is a long way off, but completes our trio of landmarks.

Watch for a sign-post on the right, ‘ Footpath to Mickleham ’ ; a path goes from here, keeping parallel to the road, descends and ascends again, and comes down finally at the entrance to Happy Valley. But a far pleasanter path goes steeply uphill to the right of this, and gives a view which is one of the best in Surrey—and very little known. This is the route I recommend. The view is more typical of Scotland. Carry on to the lane, look for a ‘ Bridle Path ’ sign, and then keep right, where there is a second notice ; these are all put up by the National Trust. Keep along the right hedge and still follow the sign until forked paths are met. Here take the left fork. Coming down to a road, turn left, keeping a wall on your right for about half a mile where, at the finish of the wall, there is a track—pile-driven to prevent wheel traffic—which starts the way to Happy Valley.

Keep right at an early fork, and carry on for a couple of miles in a beautiful valley. I counted ten magpies in pairs along this path when I was there last. At the top of the incline, bear right with the path, and you will come to the hut colony on top of Boxhill, a swimming pool and refreshment bar. To the right of the tea-place, a path runs downhill and forks right within a few yards. Keep on this or the parallel path on the slopes. It is a magnificent picture from here. Do not go down the hill, but make towards the top again, under the trees, and watch for the look-out stone erected to the memory of Leopold Salamons, who gave Boxhill to the nation. This gives directions and distances of most things seen from the summit. It seems strange that Reigate Park is only five miles as the crow flies, but we have come a long way round.

Get back to the road for a few yards, and turn left just after the Fort Tea Rooms, along a silver-birch avenue. Keep along the edge of the hill. Somewhere about here is a stone showing that a man was buried upside down : why, I do not know ; but it was his wish.

Now we return to Reigate and Redhill. Going down the hill, where you may occasionally see cyclists pushing their machines to the top, make for the most obvious tracks leading to Burford Bridge Hotel (seen through the trees). Keep near the left hedge, and while still thirty yards from a wooden fence note an almost concealed path (left). Do not miss this, as it leads to one of the best walks in the district. The path goes by the river Mole, where it is more like a Derybyshire river, and ends at the Stepping Stones. With your back to the stones, go along by a fence on your right, and bear right whenever possible. At a junction of paths, turn right, go along the road, then under the railway bridge, and cross the Mole again to the road.

This is the 'bus route to Reigate (No. 414); but you may finish the walk by crossing over to a coach-road opposite (by the golf-links). Turning left at the end, over Brockham Green towards two public-houses, take a path over a foot-bridge, keeping forward to a road and turning right to the Red Lion, Betchworth. Here we catch the same 'bus, after a walk through some of the best scenery that Surrey has to offer. The whole walk is of some sixteen miles of hilly country; by getting the 'bus opposite the coach-road it is about fourteen.

NOTE.—If you want to make two halves of this walk, break off at Headley and walk through the woods back to Walton Heath (two miles) where the No. 406 'bus comes from Epsom. There is also a London 'bus half a mile nearer (by the church) at Walton-on-the-Hill.

II. UNKNOWN TRACKS IN THE WEALD

Mercers Farm, Brewer St. Godstone, Outwood, Burstow Park.

THIS walk has the great advantage that, within a few minutes of leaving the station, you are well away on a footpath. From Redhill station go under the railway bridge towards Redstone Hill, and at the first turning—Cavendish Road—go along to the end, keeping right at the first fork, left at the second, and then continue on to the other side of the railway. Here the country opens out, and you will feel that you have really started on the day's walk, even after only this short distance.

Keep straight ahead, ignoring a right-hand path, and you will come out to a road ; turn right, and just beyond some cottages there is a lane. Go along this lane until it becomes a path and veers to the right of a cricket pitch. Pass a cottage that seems to have dropped out of a page from Dickens; and, on to a turning towards the hills, the road forks. Take the right fork, and just between a cottage and a pond a gate admits us to our next diversion.

This footpath from the gate is not too distinct, but by keeping near the hedge and looking for a house beyond (there are usually plenty of haystacks around it) and following a cart-track you can hardly go wrong. Cross the stile near the cottage, which you do not pass, and take the continuing lane. When the path rises and meets a cross-path, bear left to a stile. In a few minutes you reach a road and see the gates of Pendell Court. Have a look at the lake through the gate, but turn right for a few yards along the road. A stile by a notice-board shows you your path and you will see Pendell Court as you go along. It is a very fine house. The Virginian creeper was a glorious red when I saw it and the tall graceful chimneys gave it a noble appearance.

Cross the road and opposite is your next stile. Take the path by the right-hand hedge. Then go left and across a gravelly path towards a white cottage, but do not go over the stile at the right of the house ; you will find one well to the left with another path running to it, along by some railings. Cross over the ditch and, meeting a top path, turn left again. You will come into Brewer Street. If you are a lover of old houses you will enjoy yourself here.

Take the sign-posted road to Godstone for half a mile and just before it swings right look in a corner between two roads for the footpath. This is a very simple and plainly marked path—perhaps because it is the nearest way to an inn. It wheels round a field and, becoming a cart-track, emerges on to a road, carries on over the road, and, at the end, turns left for Godstone.

Godstone, I consider, is the best place in Surrey for any kind of refreshment. In the worst days of the war I have known parties who have forgotten to book beforehand, but tea has always been obtained. There are places well outside the hub of the village which are incomparable. Cobbett once went to Godstone and described the gardens as 'very pretty.'

'Walker' Miles, the 'patron saint' of walkers, is buried in Godstone churchyard, and his grave is easily found at the back of the church. You will probably be here again on another walk, so take the East Grinstead road and, in about a mile, fork right to the road sign-posted to Blechingley.

In between the two roads is an upward path to Tilburstow Hill. Ascend it and bear right at the top. It has an outlook over agricultural country and is fairly rugged in character. Just near the end, after passing an open space, and twenty or thirty yards from the white posts and road, a path runs down the hill to another path, at which you turn right and carry on until North Lodge gate is reached.

Here you turn left down an almost unused

path. You may find bamboo canes have overgrown the actual way in places, and even barbed wire which has been forgotten by the Military. In order to avoid the house (Underhills) go left and then right at the first turning, going by some glass-houses and then, round the farm, out on to the road. Turn left there and go through to South Park estate. In this estate is possibly the smallest church in Surrey. It was originally (1909) a stable, and is a daughter-church of St. Marks, Blechingley. Inside is a book giving many particulars relating to its history. We culled from this work that in 1401 a park-keeper was given threepence a day : 120 years later it was raised to fourpence : but it gives no later records.

Continue along the road past the church and look back at the fine Elizabethan chimney. In a few minutes the road becomes a bridle-path, and this is followed until the chimneys of commerce loom ahead to strike an incongruous note. Here we turn right and follow the wheel-tracks. Keep forward at a fork and, coming to a gate, pass through the grounds of Homestead. In front is a barn which has been transformed into a billiard room ; it is very elaborate, and the whole house charms the eye in passing on to the road.

Turn right past Fidlers Grove at the end of

the lane. Do not go beyond the pond, but turn in right at a gate by the hedge (Harewood Park), and over another gate on the left. Half-right across the field is a stile, but the path is not apparent. Now bear right to another stile and keep along the farther hedge. There is only a permissive path along a well-marked track to a farm on the left, the proper route being along to the right of this, though it is badly marked. But it is only two or three fields to the road, and more than one stile to help you.

On reaching the road turn left for Outwood and The Bell inn, which will be your first introduction to the village, with the two windmills just behind it ; one of the two claims to be the oldest in the country. Look around the green, and go along a path by the sign-post which leads to a cricket ground.

Take a left path from the ground, which will lead to Lloyd Hall. There is a tea-place just to the left of this exit, and it is your only opportunity near here for refreshment.

Take this same road back past the hall for half a mile to the church and, just before reaching it, turn in at a lane which leads round the church to the back of it, bearing left and continuing as a newly made-up road to a gate. On getting over the gate, go forward along a hedge. Ahead you will see a cluster of houses, after the second field has been negotiated. This is Burstow Park where, after passing the gates, turn left-hand, and at a pond go half-right across the field, towards a house near the corner. There is no visible path, but a stile at the end.

Go right at the road and, just after crossing a small stream, there is a way that is difficult to trace ; it is better to go farther along the road, opposite a red dairy-shed, where a more marked path goes across to Crabhill farm. This passes by the backs of houses and through fields, coming out by a pond where you turn right. At the sign-post—a few yards on—proceed left. You are near South Nutfield station, but as the service is poor it is better to continue past the church and at Kingsmill Manor (which is worth a second glance) go on by the Redhill road (sign-post), until a humped bridge is reached. Just beyond this a stile indicates the way (left).

It comes out to the Philanthropic Society's grounds where it is possible to make an interesting deviation by going under the railway. Bear right along a path at the back of the master's house, and follow this same path over a field beside a stream, finishing at the Earlswood Institution. Then the way is by a gate opposite, under a railway arch, along an avenue of trees, and on to the main Redhill road.

If you do not make this detour, carry

straight on past the small church, out to the cemetery, and past the gasometer into Redhill. The distance is about fifteen miles, but there is a lot of variety in the walk, which covers some of the most interesting country around Redhill.

III. MAINLY BY THE MOLE

Redhill Common, Reigate Park, Flanchford Farm, Betchworth, Brockham Green, Boxhill, Betchworth Kilns, Lower Pilgrim's Way, Colley Hill.

FROM Redhill station turn along by the traffic-lights and then go left along the Brighton Road. At the cinema on the right, go along Lower Bridge Road, and where it forks go left uphill (Upper Bridge Road); cross over the main road to a footpath going over Redhill Common. Keep forward on the sandy track, and in a few yards the view begins to open out. It is a fine panorama. Farther along, the church of St. John shows up on the left, with a ringed plateau which might have been a fairies' ring. The path ends at a junction of paths and a gate. Proceed through the gate for a few yards, and turn left at Hightrees Road. At Dunottar School keep left, and continue along this suburban road until it ends; when a few yards left, a continuing path by the side of a drive will lead to a surprisingly pretty walk. The tall, graceful pines sloping down on one side give it quite a Scottish accent. Keep on this path, till between houses another path on the left is reached, and where this emerges keep on and you will reach a narrow lane and gate. The gate is on our route, which passes a huge sand-pit.

Follow this path to the old Brighton Road and turn right to a crossing beacon by the park gates. Reigate walkers would join up here, coming from the station along Tunnel Road and Bell Street opposite. Go into the park and take the first right track in a few yards. Keep by the side of a fence through the park, as this is no ordinary corporation affair, but a place in which you can easily be lost.

Through gaps in the fence you will see Reigate Priory, where the Earl Beattie once lived, and later the lake comes into prominence. Coming out to a road, turn right past some allotments and our next path is by a wide ditch and white gate on left. You have now by-passed Reigate.

Coming out at a narrow lane, go right for a few yards and just past two cottages. Get over a stile (left). Where the next field has been ploughed up, the path runs by a cottage and round the field, keeping the same direction. Coming to a road, turn right-wards and at the fork (sign-post) left. Just before reaching a solitary cottage, the footpath starts for Flanchford farm. It becomes a bit rough near the end, but gives a fine view of the little farm. At the mill-pond there is another spot of colour. You come out to the road and go left over a bridge—crossing the river Mole.

Meditatively you gaze over the narrow bridge, and are suddenly brought to earth by a double-decker 'bus, and realise you are on the Leigh Road. Continue along this road, past the entrance to Little Flanchford farm, and in a short distance a sign-post points to a footpath (to Gadbrook) inside the garden of a house ; the field is the correct approach, but barbed wire is a menace ; so it is better to pass through the garden. You may have to step over props, but its legality is unquestioned.

The path is joined in a corner of the field by another path. Keep to the left hedge and ignore a stile on the left, but go between that and a pond with a byre just beyond. Look for a gate on the right, which is our way, before reaching a tree in the field. Standing by the gate (after closing it) count along to the fourth telegraph-pole and make for that. A dozen yards beyond the pole, a break in the wire fence gives an indication where the plank bridge lies that we are to cross. Get over the stile and swing directly right, keeping by the hedge.

You will now pass a little-known corner of the Mole. Following round the field, leave the river for a bit by bearing left-wards where, in a few yards, you will pick up a cart-track, which turns right at the end of the field then left at a black cottage, and the path becomes a cinder-track to Snower Hill farm.

On reaching the road, turn right-wards, and after the hard stubble it is plain sailing—although you are on the road for about a mile. There is more than one pretty cottage on the way, but one in particular where the road bends. The hills ahead are our ultimate objective. Pass over Betchworth Bridge. You may have been over here on a previous walk, but if not, look round the village street at the other side of the church. The Dolphin Inn may interest you too. The church lies opposite, and the walk continues through the churchyard and along the left-hand hedge, where presently the river comes to light again ; this is a very pleasant path along the river-bank, and a favourite with walkers. Near the end there is a fine vantage-point : the backward view of the Mole and a peep at Brockham church suggests a good composition for a photograph.

At the termination of the path, go left over

a bridge and then diagonally right towards a gate in the corner. You will emerge on Brockham Green, where they still play cricket. The church stands at the end of the green, and you will note there is, too, a well on the opposite green. Directly across the road we joined is another narrow road ; make for this, and in a few yards, on the right, is the old coach-road running by Betchworth golf-links. We go along this road, which starts by a lodge gate, for about a mile and a half ; it is more like a footpath as no traffic passes over it. Betchworth Castle lies to the right, but is not of any interest now.

When coming to the end of the road with three gates near each other, look for an iron rail and posts almost in front, and pass through to another path under some chestnut trees. You may find chestnuts on the ground in autumn. The path runs by the fence and down to the main road, almost opposite a swimming pool and tea-rooms. Pass down by the left of the café for a view of the mill, where, again, a camera would be useful.

Turning right-wards, we come back to the main road again, and by turning left and then left again by Pixham Grove Nurseries (sign) we come out opposite where we left the coach-road. In fact, the detour was only for snacks and snaps, and to see all the best of this corner. Along this road, over a bridge where

A BETCHWORTH FOOTPATH

we get our last glimpse of the Mole, fork left under a railway-bridge. At the end it merges into a carriage drive with two paths, one on each side. We take the right one by the side of a drive winding uphill, and, emerging at a major path, turn right-wards. There are magnificent views from this path—a lower one than that we were on in a previous walk over Boxhill. Look for the spire of Dorking church, and you can pick out Brockham also by its church. On a clear day the whole range of hills from Leith Hill can be made out, with small farms nestling in the valleys. You are actually looking along the Holmsdale valley. The river is almost lost, but here and there you may catch a glint of it in the sunshine. The 'buses on the main road look like ants crawling along. This path appears to end at a corner, and where it goes backwards look for a scrambling bit. Proceed through the bushes and on downhill for about fifty yards, where your route will be crossed by a larger, precipitous path, downhill on the right, which we take.

When in sight of the railway and open field, you will see another path on the left, lined by yews. This is our route now, and, according to some authorities, it is part of the Pilgrim's Way. At a fork, keep left—the other way leads to the Barley Mow Inn. In a short distance, the lime-kilns are passed, then the steps which lead to a path beyond them, under a small bridge. Suddenly, the path appears to open up into mountainous country, for ahead are the hills which seem to tower above the walker.

Keep downhill along the valley until well along the woods, where a backward path leads uphill to the plateau above. Continue, and this will cut off a corner and lead to the exit by a row of houses. If you miss this path, you will come out by the rails and tracks of the lime-kiln and meet the road to Betchworth station. In either case turn left. In about three-quarters of a mile, just beyond a double bend, look for a house called Pebble-down and a path just beyond with white fencing. Proceed along this until it enters a field, then go uphill on the left to a copse. When almost at the top, turn right-wards. This is the Lower Pilgrim's Way, so long a bone of contention with the owners and Reigate Borough Council, but now happily restored as a public right-of-way.

The way lies through a grove and by palings to a junction of paths. Here, cross over, and go up the incline to another fence of palings in the same direction. These soon develop into two rows, and we pass between them. When coming into the open country, where the view is good, keep near the hedge, and the path by the palings is picked up again. This path is not very wide, and at the side are dense masses of bushes and trees. We pass on our left an inviting path, which leads to Walton Heath.

Proceeding along a tunnel darkened by a wealth of overhanging trees, an uncanny eeriness steals over you. Probably it is aroused by the denseness of the yew trees. A slight turn right brings the path to two gates, but do not pass beyond them ; advance along the wire fence up the slope, turning leftwards over the stubble, and proceed to the copse, well over on your left. The path is not distinct, but the only opening is high up the slope and, as barbed wire surrounds the field, it is imperative to connect with this.

Having negotiated this, the continuation is easy. Turn right and follow the side of the field, where a rough path may be distinguished. At a junction of three paths, take the middle one, and go forward. Keeping to this track, and avoiding all paths uphill or down to fields, we arrive at some steps and a lovely little dell, which we can make a note of for future exploration. It contains a spring, and is a charming place for a picnic, but being at the end of our journey we can only give it a glance.

Colley Hill now comes into view, and we soon arrive at the green barrier by the Pilgrim's Way. Continue to the Yew Tree inn, or turn right at the first turning and then left. Either way will bring you to Reigate station, after a fifteen-mile walk, much of which has been by the Mole.

IV. ON THE SUSSEX BORDER

Crawley, Ifield, Rusper, Russ Hill, Charlwood, Farmfield, Hookwood, Horley.

A WALK may be planned from Redhill which, by keeping near the borders, includes a certain amount of Sussex and Surrey. This walk is near the county boundary, and will include some of the villages just beyond Surrey. If arriving by Green Line, stay in the 'bus till the end of the journey, otherwise get a No. 405 'bus from Redhill to Crawley.

From Reigate, it is better to change at Redhill, or if you like a run round the countryside there is a 'bus which starts from Reigate (No. 424) to Horley, and then you can change there.

The No. 405 'bus goes *via* Earlswood, Salfords, Horley, then past Gatwick race-course (left), which has had a very quiet time this past six or seven years; then on the right-hand side look out for the mill at Lowfield Heath.

There is a footpath way from Lowfield

Heath, but at the time of writing a bridge had broken down, and instead of repairing it the path had been more or less blocked in the hope that it would be forgotten. So, instead of taking other paths which would probably have suited us, we prefer to start from Crawley.

This is the town where, during a farcical race to Brighton, the competitors were asked to crawl on their hands and knees while going through the town. Thus was humour satisfied—at least to the promoters. Have a look round the town, and observe the bird on the church-tower. It was a very busy town in the old coaching days, and still has plenty to offer the motorist and walker in the way of inns.

To start our walk, take the Horsham road (Ifield Road), and keep to the right-hand road at a fork by a church. There is a queer statue at the corner of a children's recreation ground. It is a bearded man holding a lady with a broken leg, but nobody seems sure of its *raison d'être* or origin.

Just after a double-bend sign, look out for a road to the left which has a notice, 'No through road.' Along this road, in about fifty yards, there is an iron gate, which starts our path. We shall see the by-pass road ahead, as we go by the cemetery. Go over or under the bar which acts as a stile, on the right, and then turn sharp left under the by-pass road.

The path proceeds through a field opposite the tunnel, and emerges at a road—just above Ifield railway station.

Turn right-wards and again right at the major road in a few yards. Shortly, Ifield church looms up in the picture and, where the road bends, a sign points the way to the Plough inn. It is a pretty corner, and the church lies at the end. The church is worth a visit.

It contains the largest organ-blower (in a box) the writer has ever seen, and a screen made from the wood of an oak tree which grew at Lowfield Heath, known as the County Oak. It used to be said that Sussex alone could supply enough oak to build all the navies of Europe. That, of course, was when all ships were made of wood.

Whether you call at the Plough or not, keep left-wards round it, passing the cricket ground on your right. The footpath next to the back entrance of The Old Rectory is our route, and, crossing a tiny bridge over a ditch, it becomes a field-path. Take the right of two bridges at the end of the field, and here it may be muddy.

Look ahead for two telegraph-poles, make for the left-hand one by a corner of the next field, and pass through a gateway there. Turn right-wards to a house, facing you, where a white wicket-gate leads through the woods. You will be lucky if you arrive here in blackberry time. On coming to a road, turn left-wards past some quaint wooden houses, and, reaching a bend in the road, look in the right-hand corner, by a cottage garden, where there is a stile, almost hidden. Be careful to choose the correct gate : there are two, and though there does not appear to be a foot-path, it is a right-of-way. On the right of the two gates, keep to the right-hand hedge for one field and, coming to a normal stile, you will feel more reassured as the path becomes plainer. But be careful when getting over this stile : there may be a large hole covered by grass.

Proceed in the same direction over the next field, and at a dip on the right the path merges into a cross-track with wire netting on one side. Turn left-wards between netting and ditch. Here the view opens up, and we can see in the distance the trees of St. Leonard's Forest. This track is not used very much, but it is easy to follow, through a gate-way towards a black building and the road. Directly opposite is a stile and, having got over that, look for the telegraph-lines and follow them half-right from the stile to the corner of the field. If crops are growing, you may have to go round the field, but make for a gate leading into a lane.

Continue past a house called The Mount ;

this is a beautiful example of what Sussex can sometimes show us. Along the lane are woods which are, of course, at their best in springtime. Arriving at a pond on the right, do not take either of the two roads ahead, but go straight forward to a stile which is almost hidden behind bushes and between the two roads. This awkward stile, approached by a ditch, starts another path not well marked. Proceed for about fifty yards, and the path is crossed by another coming from a house. Turn left-wards along this, and drop to the gap in the hedge of the first field, almost opposite a galvanised-iron building. Directly you get into this field, turn sharp right—there is no visible path and a barricade of wooden poles (in *lieu* of a stile) indicates the way over a stream by a path marked by pig-netting.

You will have noticed the fine prospect before going under the trees. This is a captivating path, and is worth some trouble to find. A gate opposite, when coming into the open, shows the continuance of the path, and the wall and garden of Venters is our next objective. Now look ahead for an inclined path, slightly left, near the hedge and approached by a small bridge. This is a picturesque corner, and here one could rest a little and let the beauty of the scene sink in. Follow the netting, and by keeping the hedge on your right and passing stiles and gates all the way to Rusper, you will come out at a small telephone-exchange.

Some day somebody will discover Rusper, but until that day arrives let us enjoy it undisturbed.

There are two inns here, a church with the tidiest churchyard you will ever see, and a number of delightful houses. We have passed the rear of one of the largest houses on our footpath approach, and a peep through the gates, which will probably be open, might be forgiven. Go into the churchyard for the view, which is an unusual one of the Leith Hill range, seen over to the right. This general view is one of the best for miles round.

With your back to the Star, proceed up the street and take the right-hand fork ; on your left through the trees you may get a peep at a squat-looking tower. On the right is a farm and further still on the right is a stile and path. This leads to Orltons, and is a little-known path which deserves to be used more often. Hugging the hedge on our left, we pass through a copse, and here the outlook is very fine. You may disturb a hare or even a fox, but it would be a real surprise if you found another human being. Two more fields are crossed ; pass a corner stile to Orltons, and keep along the lane ; you have just crossed over to Surrey.

Where the road bends, look for a stile on the right and take a path—hardly distinct—half-left, to the corner of the field near a road. There is a gap with iron rails on one side, and the path goes near the hedge. There are sometimes obstacles in the way of this path. Further on, the left-hand hedge is changed for one on the right ; then comes a field where you may have to pick your way through cabbages, or other crops, to a gap and gate opposite. This continues as a cart-track through an orchard.

Keep right at the approach to a poultry-farm, on the way to Russ Hill, where there is a path leading through Glovers Wood, nearly opposite, but this is not recommended. It is better to carry on down the hill until four roads cross at Windacres farm (you will have to look back to see the name). Take a path between the two left-hand roads, passing a cottage on the right and coops on the left, going uphill.

This is a well-marked and easy path to follow, and the way leads to Charlwood church. It goes round one field, across another, and over a grass road, and presently the church can be seen with the path finishing almost at the door.

Charlwood church is one of the most interesting in Surrey, and there are faint traces of mural decorations. It is said to date from

1082, and there is a fine old chest which contains records showing how they used to use a number of nails before weights had been standardised. The marks on the porch door were made by the pikemen as they sharpened their pikes. Tea is possible at local inns.

Go through the village, and look at the view of the church from the post-office. Just beyond an ironmonger's shop there is a road, Chapel Road. Before proceeding along it, you may care to know that a 'bus goes from Charlwood to Horley every two hours, and to Crawley the alternate hours.

However, we go along the road leading to the chapel, which we presently pass, and on reaching a green lane on the left we take the path opposite, on the right. This leads to some farm-buildings, and on to a gate and stile. Watch for these stiles, and you will eventually arrive at the rear of some houses. Passing between them and a shelter, look for a lodge on the right, keeping well to the left of it. This brings us to a made-up path running to Farmfield School, and is a public footpath (left).

At the fork, take the right-hand road almost up to a white post, where an iron gate introduces another path which, at the second stile, goes round a field and becomes a cart-track, finally emerging by a garage.

There is a café here if you have not had tea.

A 'bus for Reigate goes every half-hour from the Black Horse, Hookwood, a quarter of a mile to your left ; but if you are going back by Green Line, or to Redhill, go 200 yards right to a gate on the left (with a notice by Surrey C.C.), and on the right is a footpath to Horley church. Passing some houses, watch for a right-hand track before reaching the river. The path ends at a stile on the main Brighton road. The church is a few yards further on, and there is another stile leading by the back of the church to The Six Bells, one of the oldest and most picturesque inns in the district. The 'buses, at the time of writing, went at ten minutes past and twenty to the hour. The Six Bells is opposite the back of the church. You have covered twelve to thirteen miles.

V. TO THE DERBY ON FOOT

Batts Hill, Gatton Park, Monkswell, Kingswood, Burgh Heath, Epsom Race Course, Headley Heath, Brockham, Betchworth.

IT may have been their misfortune for some people to have walked *home* from the Derby, but if you choose the way suggested here you will find it a very delightful walk.

From Redhill station, go along past the

traffic-lights to Warwick Road and Batts Hill, as in Walk I, but pass the footpath you took then and continue up the hill until it bends round. Here carry straight on by a footpath in the corner (sign-post), in a very quick way out of the town. Almost opposite, over a lane, is a continuation to a road, where, bearing left for about 200 yards, you turn into the drive by a lodge-gate (Gatton Park). Reigate walkers would join up at this entrance gate, too, making for Wray Common by Croydon Road and Gatton Road to the lodge.

The park is full of fine old trees, and lakes adorn its grounds, while the Pilgrim's Way lies to its north. One of the lakes soon appears on the right before the house becomes visible. Later on, another lake—or it may be part of the first—is also passed, and the call of a coot may be heard from its banks. Take the left cross-road, but, if time is not pressing, walk up to the old town hall, where, in the days of the Rotten Boroughs, one person could elect two members of Parliament.

Go back to the cross-roads, if you have wandered, and when it enters the road by a lodge-gate go straight over the Reigate Hill-Merstham road to a steep hill in front. Go along Babylon Lane (sign-posted to Kingswood), where the first footpath on the right goes round some farm-buildings. Avoid the paths, but take the lane straight ahead, and where a left path appears take the one nearly opposite, on the right, and along a wire fence. This path goes a good part of our way, and it is sign-posted, or has stiles, so that there is no occasion to give other information. We pass a tea-house called Monkswell.

The way continues by Kingswood golf-course, in the same direction. The approach is upwards, and the view from the top embraces all the fine country around. Shortly afterwards, the path becomes fenced-in on both sides ; we cross the road and go by one or two bungalows, then left-wards at a road, bearing right at the end, to Kingswood station. There is an opportunity for refreshment over the bridge.

Continue along the shopping road from the inn, and at the end of Waterhouse Lane cross the main road, go fifty yards right, and across the road to a path over the heath. In a few yards take a left fork (this is Burgh Heath). Keep on this path over all other forks ; it runs by a hedge and crosses a main path. Then go along the one which says 'No Horses.' This leads to a substantial stile (sign-post), and brings you into suburbia. It was once a footpath, but the outskirts of Epsom have encroached.

By a belt of trees along Shawley Way, a footpath runs off to the right by the edge of a

ield. Keep left at the fork, which leads
:hrough a wood, and bear left again at the end
road). This will bring you to Epsom Downs,
ι few yards higher up. The direction-plate
which says 'Tattenham Corner' may give
you a thrill if your memories are of races seen
ιt that spot, but the sight of the Downs, with
ιardly a spectator to share it with, may give
you another kind of sensation. Look towards
London, and, on a fine day, you may pick out
vell-known landmarks.

When ready to resume, make for the left of
he grandstand. Keep close to the stands,
uided by the posts on the left. You can see
Headley church in the distance, looking along
he line of a fence. Here you may resume a
loser acquaintance with the turf which has
nade equestrian history. The path is quite
listinguishable, and, looking back, you will
et another peep at a desolate arena before
assing a few houses and ascending the track.

Coming out to open country, bear right-
vards. Opposite is Nohome farm ; but half-
ight here is a little-used path leading to a
ıne, an old Roman road, and ending opposite
 lodge-gate.Enter the park by a gate at the
ide, and go over a left stile, then along to a
oad ; bear right for 200 yards, past a few
nodern cottages, and take another left path
which finishes at Headley church. There are
nany epitaphs in the churchyard.

From Headley church, take a lower path sign-posted to the village ; continue left by the road, cutting off a corner by another sign-post, and continue between pond and house. This is Headley Heath, and the road dwindles to a path (started by two stumps). Keep on this path for half a mile, and, where it joins a cross-path, keep left, going towards the west. Look for a dip in the distant landscape, and work to the left of it. If you manage this correctly you will pass through some beautiful birch trees and bracken. The house above is High Ashurst, and the valley below is full of interest. Cross the valley at any of the paths, and on the other side of the hill is a lane. Keep well left of High Ashurst and go along the valley some way before ascending. You are bound to strike the lane which forks ; take the right fork and cross the road. You are near the top of Boxhill, but carry on to a continuing path which becomes precipitous on its way to Brockham Lane.

There is a 'bus from here to Reigate and Redhill (No. 414), but if time permits there is a left path before reaching the railway-bridge which will take you to The Barley Mow Inn or to Betchworth station, about two miles further. After doing the fourteen miles from Redhill you may feel the 'bus is preferable.

FARTHING DOWNS

VI. 'TWIXT KENT AND SURREY AND THE PILGRIM'S WAY

Nutfield, Castle Hill, Blechingley, Garston, Godstone, Gibbs Brook, Tandridge, Oxted, Titsey Hill, Woldingham, Marden Park, Caterham, Quarry Hangers, Merstham.

THERE is a choice of two ways for the start of this walk. If you like to miss the preliminary bit of getting beyond the town, and prefer to commence the day by getting as near to the first footpath as possible, take a 'bus from Reigate or Redhill (Nos. 410 and 411) which will drop you at Nutfield school. Here the road opposite (sign-post 'South Nutfield ') gives us our start, and where the road forks take the centre footpath.

Should you disdain the 'bus and prefer to walk all the way, the same spot can be reached by a very pleasant by-way. From Redhill station, go under the railway-bridge, and continue up Redstone Hill on the road until, near the top, you pass Redstone Hollow. Just beyond this road a gap in the hedge (right) leads past a house. While not a footpath in the sense that we understand it, there is a fair stream of people going through this short-cut, and it has a very fine view, showing Redhill in a hollow and, flanking it, all the hills which go to make the town such a delightful place. You may pick out the Pilgrim's Way on Colley Hill.

Pass by the house, with its broken windows, keeping left downhill through the glade into Woodland Way. At the end of this road turn left-wards uphill by a road which, being high up, gives other vistas of surprising charm. At a fork, keep left, passing parts of a cemetery on the right ; the winding road eventually turns through typical Surrey scenery, and, crossing the South Nutfield road, goes forward to a continuing road. This passes under the lee of Nutfield Priory, which may be seen on the left above the highway.

Coming to the road sign-posted to Nutfield, turn left again. If you are not afraid of mud, take a path across the allotments almost opposite, bear left, and then drop downhill to a farm. The path runs in front of this farm and along by the recreation ground, the goal-posts of which may be used as a guide to locate it. But as the ground here is always very muddy it is far better to stick to where a path runs parallel with another road on the right ; this is the junction of the route for those coming by 'bus to Nutfield school.

At Nutfield village, keep along to a baker's shop, where a path runs uphill along the left of it. Should you have had the temerity to try the muddy footpath, you would have to turn left at the exit of Nutfield recreation-ground, and the baker's shop would be found in the middle of the village. Nutfield is quite worth looking over, and has photographic possibilities.

The path leads to an inclined path through a wood. This comes into open fields, with a view of sweeping downs. Below, in the valley, the main road is lost to sight. Coming to a road, turn left for a few yards ; go up a drive by a cottage and, just before reaching the house, bear right round some outbuildings, where milking may be in progress ; then, coming to a holly tree, turn right again and go along by a fence. On looking up, Castle Hill may be seen ahead, and by taking the first path on the left with a double row of rails, ascend this hilly avenue to the old castle walls.

There is a seat at the summit where you can survey the Weald below. There is a view on the right, framed by a tree, which is a picture for any discriminating photographer. There are ponds in the front and bright little lodges which captivate the eye and hold the attention by their beauty.

The end of this path leads to another, but if you are in search of an interesting village—and refreshment—or even if you are not, Blechingley is only a few yards above, and is a village you should not miss. (It is sometimes spelt Bletchingley.) Blechingley has a church with an enormous family monument covering a whole chancel wall.

After picking up the footpath again, turn right at the road, go beyond some cottages, and then left along a lane fringed by a pond. This becomes a path through a copse. The path continues as a road on approaching a house, and keeps to the ridge of a hill, passing cottages and wandering round a field. Look for a half-timbered house on the right, where the path comes into a road again. Turn up this (left), and continue uphill to a cross-road. At the end of the road get over a stile opposite and take the path past a house with a lovely outlook (Garston House).

The lake and old mill-house, after coming through the drive and turning right, are picturesque items in a very varied walk, which now comes out to Godstone Green. There are caves in Godstone, near the 'bus garage, but as walkers have been known to lose themselves all day before finding their way out we are not recommending them.

We have been to Godstone on a previous walk, and may refresh our memory. Here the Clayton Arms has been renamed ; formerly it was the White Harte.

Take the East Grinstead road, go past a few cottages, and keep left at a fork. At the end of these cottages, turn left for twenty yards. A stile on the right takes us over a field dropping down to a road. Take the lane opposite, and carry on past the rear of a house, taking the first path beyond that (right). The path goes between two ponds, and brings you to Leigh Place (Gibbs Brook). Straight ahead, we emerge on to another lane and turn left. At this point, there is a small waterfall. Go over the small bridge, and through a wood—a lovely bit of colour in October—into a field and the open country. The path is distinct, and comes out by The Barley Mow.

Turn left here, and take the road for half a mile, then turn right at the road-junction, and Tandridge church is just round the corner. Go in by lych-gate, and see one of the finest yew trees in Surrey. The yew tree has been estimated to have lived for 1,000 years in some parts.

Beyond the church-approach there is another path running by a wall and over the tarred lane to a golf-links. Make for the golf-house, turn right at the main road, and drop into Oxted. At the end of the town, fork left and go up the main shopping-centre to the railway-station. Go under the station by the subway; turn right again at the exit, past more shops, then left by the Westminster Bank, opposite a green. Take the first turning on the right and, ignoring the first footpath on left, take the second—which is opposite a footpath running towards Limpsfield, a place to explore on some other occasion.

This sandy path leads to a road through a gate with view of the hills beyond. Do not worry about the notice on the gate, as the footpath is a right-of-way along the hedge to a swing-gate and a stile. Go through a copse, and left by the edge of the wood. Gradually go uphill by the side of a fine wood and, getting near the top, take a rest and look back—if you have not already done so. You will be well repaid. The scene below is practically the same as the one from Titsey Hill, which is not far away. When near the top, bear left to the other side of the field. There is more than one path to the top left-hand corner, but on reaching the road go right past Whistlers Steep. Go to the top of the hill and the road-junction. If there is plenty of time, the view from farther along the road by some chalk cliffs is worth seeking. Continue by Whistlers Woods (a house) and pass Whistlers Warren. Keep forward, ignoring a path going to a water-tower, but looking at the sweep of country in that direction. This path comes out above Woldingham, the village being reached in about a mile (left-wards at road).

At the village green, go round the right-hand side. On facing a 'bus-shelter, continue round the bend of the green to the left—not by the main road—to a house named Haverbrack (about 500 yards). Be sure to take in the two sides of the green. Here a footpath runs by the side of the house. This is a pleasant path over hills, and bears slightly right over a railway-bridge. It gives fine views, and finishes by a paddock where a sign guides you on. Although there may be no visible path by this sign, go through a gate on the opposite side of the field, keeping level with the left hedge, which helps to locate the way. Under the trees, on the same line of direction, there is another gate, and uphill we view the landscape. The road we have just crossed leads to Marden Park (left), but there are rights-of-way through it. Keep forward by a copse and through some fields. Just before reaching a farm, look for Caterham church spire, and turn along the path by the gate. On coming to some rifle-butts, on the right, the route is by the distinct path to the farm ahead. Pass Tillingdown farm, and go on by a pond to the lane and by-pass road. Cross, and in the direction of the church, not plainly visible, there is a path running down to a recreation-ground. There are 121 or 122 steps to negotiate—see how many *you* make it.

Here is Caterham, a café and a way back by 'bus or train for anyone who has not time to finish the walk. Just beyond the railway-station is Harestone Valley Road ; turn up this, and keep left at the fork. A mile of road now, but it is inevitable in a large centre like Caterham. There are three ways through Tupwood, but this is the quickest and probably the prettiest. Keep left at a fork and right at the end of the road. Passing a wood, resist the temptation to enter, as it leads to Godstone, and keep along this road towards a tower. At the sign 'To Surrey Crest,' bear left and right again round a fence. At the next sign ('The tea place in 1 min.'), keep left along a path on the edge, and continue through to the end—coming to Whitehills. Continue up Whitehill Lane—one of the most lovely of Surrey's leafy lanes—and finish at a tower which was used for fire-watching.

Our continuing path is almost opposite, but the Harrow Inn is only a few yards further on. Ignore a left-hand footpath, and continue along this farm-track, bearing left at a junction, crossing a road, and going uphill. Here swing left, and go to the top of the hill, where a path shows plainly over the Quarry Hangers. Keep on the top as long as you can, descending by a left path, and come out by some cottages.

This is along the Pilgrim's Way, and the views are very effective. The pilgrims are supposed to have used as high a point as possible, principally to avoid interference and damp conditions, but you will probably find mud in some of the tracks hereabouts. On reaching the road, go right where Rockshaw Road runs into Merstham, by the church. You are then only a couple of miles above Redhill, and 'buses and trains are available if you need them. Your walk has been a hilly fifteen miles.

An alternative route from Godstone through Marden Park for those who wish to shorten the route is as follows:

Go through the yard of the Clayton Arms to a path passing some lakes. On coming to the church, turn left to the main road, coming out opposite Ouborough. A lane almost opposite will lead to the park gate, but a better way is to look for a path running by the side of a cottage along this lane, and, mounting the track, ascend a hill breaking into the park at the top (left).

It is difficult to describe the actual entrance to the park at the moment of writing, as the Army have been operating there, but use your discretion at the top of the hill.

This path runs through some beautiful woodland, and drops down near the house. Continue by the park road (right), past a house, and fork left at the lodge. The farm here has some of the earliest snowdrops in the spring, and the path continues over the Downs to Tillingdown farm.

This will shorten the route by a good three miles.

VII. TOWARDS LEITH HILL

Redhill Common, Earlswood Common, Petridge Woods, Sidlow Bridge, Leigh, Parkgate, Newdigate, Reffolds Copse, Beare Green.

STARTING from the traffic-lights, walk along Brighton Road until the first cross-roads are reached, then turn up Mill Street and take the first left-hand path (uphill); cross over, and take one going more sedately along the valley, keeping right as far as you are able, and scrambling to the top at the finish. Here the trees are particularly fine; bear left and, still ascending, you will reach a commemoration stone. From here you see to the left the church of St. John, while in the mid-distance are Earlswood Lakes.

As these are our objective you may work out your direction. A good way is to take the main path which runs from the right towards a chimney-stack, past the 'bus-shelter, and over the road. There is then a path over the grass which keeps the lakes in view for the best part of the time. As the lakes are divided we may walk between them, making for the further right-hand corner (the south-west).

Here is a road (Woodhatch-Salfords) and beside the last cottage is the footpath to Petridge Woods. This common is used as part of the Redhill golf-course.

Keep to the main track through the woods, coming out at Lonesome Lane; then left until, just after crossing a bridge opposite another cottage, the path goes by a stream right-wards. This stream is the overflow from Gatton Lakes, and it joins the Mole a little later at Sidlow Bridge, which we cross and come to the Old Brighton Road from Reigate.

Our way is by a gate opposite and along a hedge, where a gap after a quarter of a mile gives a sight of a pair of cottages and a path (right) leading to them. Turn left at the road, or if you have been to see Sidlow church you would have passed through Iron's Bottom and joined us here; go on by some cottages until a lodge on the right with a notice, 'Private Road—No thoroughfare,' points the way along a drive. Just before a white gate, take a left path and then a right path, to avoid the house in front.

Follow this lane to the walled garden of Bury's Court, where there are three ways to Leigh: out to the road by a drive, straight on by a farm, or round left by a barn and path to Leigh Place. If you elect to go by the road, bear left at all turnings and you pass the moated house of Leigh Place (the second way is the better). Leigh is a village to linger in. The footpaths are being watched by the Women's Institute and a live parish council. If you have only a short time to spare, 'buses run back to Reigate and Redhill.

To continue the walk, go along the Betchworth road past some houses and a school, and then past the Seven Stars inn. A path starts just beyond a mission-hall on the left. Keeping close to the right hedge, go through two gates, then strike across a field to a solitary tree, keeping in line with a ditch. Cross here, and at the edge of the opposite cottages (fifty yards right) look for a hidden stile. Go forward until a byre is reached, and join the lane on the left. Do not wander over the fields beyond, thinking there is a better way out, as a brook stops you. Go along this lane, beyond the barn and over a gate. In the right-hand corner there is another gate by some hay-ricks. Keep along here, and cross over to a parellel path on the other side of the ditch on the left, keeping on in the same direction. This sounds rather involved, but owing to an alteration in paths it is the better way. At a broken fence, a quarter of a mile ahead, bear left through a copse, left again down a dip, and the gates of Mynthurst are ahead. (They had been knocked down when I was there.)

Turn sharp right, almost back whence you

came, and proceed just beyond Mynthurst Old Farm (left), to some farm-buildings ; go through, turn right for 200 yards, and then take a left lane. Proceed along this to a pond, and follow the cart-tracks through a gap. Strike half-left to the lower of two paths (by trees), and carry on. Go over the gate, by a pond, but do not go as far as the bungalow in front, but over a gate to the left ; now go straight on.

If it becomes very muddy, strike off to the right over the heath to the road ; otherwise keep straight on to another road which, by turning right, arrives at the same spot. This is Parkgate, with the Surrey Oaks and a cricket ground just beyond the cross-roads towards Newdigate. You will pass some lovely old cottages along this road with some queer names, Ratcatchers Cottage being one, just round a corner. In about a mile on the right is a house, Meadowview, with a long approach. Next to it is our footpath. As the sign is hidden from this direction, you may pass it unless you look carefully.

The path does not look inviting, but make for the left-hand corner of the field, keeping forward and in a westerly direction. It improves and brings you into a pretty wood : this is Reffolds Copse. At the meeting of three paths, take the centre one and, as this path crosses another, look for two rails (the stile) just after. The peep down the valley is enchanting, covered with rosebay willow-herb for miles. As this flower has about 400 seeds per plant to distribute, it is easy to see how it spreads through our woods.

Cross the road and go through the grounds of a lovely house, continuing by the road to Beare Green. There are tea-places here to the right and left. From the seventeenth-century tea-place on one side and the snack-bar on the other, we have variety to suit everybody.

We have managed to get near to Leith Hill, and it would be just as pleasant to go on through Kitlands or Broom Hall to the summit, but my task now is to get you back to Redhill. If you 'call it a day,' get the No. 414 'bus back to Reigate or Redhill, or if they are full (a possibility on a sunny Sunday) walk to Holmwood, a starting-point where you will be sure of a seat. There is a railway-station at Holmwood, too. There are foot-paths back to Leigh, Gadbrook and Betchworth by a quieter but less interesting way higher up the hill.

This walk has been over about twelve miles of rough country.

VIII. MORE OF THE PILGRIM'S WAY

Reigate Hill, Colley Hill, Mogador, Kingswood Church, Chipstead Valley, Hooley, Netherne, Chaldon, Merstham, Wiggie.

WE start this walk from Reigate High Street. From the old town hall, walk towards Dorking, and on the right-hand by the side of a dairy there is a path going by a few steps to the castle. Most of the castle grounds have been laid out as pleasure-gardens, but underneath, even running under the High Street shops, there are caves.

Proceeding out of the castle grounds by a pond, turn right-wards to the London Road, and continue left-wards past Reigate station. In half a mile the Yew Tree inn is passed, and just beyond there is a break between some houses on the left. After passing a few cottages and the entrance to the bird-sanctuary, bear right uphill to where a monument has been erected.

This is the Pilgrim's Way, and a landmark for many miles round, its chalky surface showing up strongly in the sunlight, and the contours of hills. At the top of the hill we pass again the mosaic fountain seen on our first walk. Turn left here, going by the same way over Colley Hill which we took to Headley.

But when abreast of the green posts, near the right hedge, notice a couple of yards beyond them a gate on the right marked 'for residents only.' This precedes a path leading to a lane, which we take. We make no apology for going over Colley Hill again, as the view is worth a second visit. Continue until a fence on the left shows a path in front going to a road (Mogador). By turning right-wards here, you reach a sign to The Sportsman inn. You may need refreshment, but if not the way lies past the inn by the hedge, keeping right at a fork. The spire of Kingswood church will be seen peeping shyly out of a wealth of trees. As this church is our objective we can hardly go wrong, but at a solitary cottage bear left for a few yards, then go forward. After passing a school the church comes close to hand, and we cross the main road to it. There are other inns to your left a few hundreh yards along the Chussex Plain.

If you go in the church you will be struck by the fine windows, with their deep colouring. There is also one of the sweetest peal of bells in Surrey. A modern touch is the use of the microphone.

Passing the church, turn right-wards between road and church, and in a few yards right again, along the Warren with its wonderful avenue of firs. This was the venue of a pitched battle which lasted for seventeen

FROM REIGATE HILL

years, when Sir John Hartopp endeavoured to enclose 1,300 acres of heath and common-land. Lord Eversley once handed me his book on the proceedings which took place (*Commons, Forests and Footpaths*), and the thanks of all walkers are due to him for the patient and persevering efforts to preserve these paths for the public.

A few yards along the Warren, a footpath on the right—our route—leads to the back of the church, goes over a lane, and continues as a road. The observant may notice near the churchyard an animals' cemetery on the right, one tombstone proclaiming that a pet 'lay in celestial sunshine.' At the end of the road, carry on to a group of buildings, and here you have a choice of ways. By the right-hand path over the golf-links, you come to a road where, by turning left-wards along it, you pass the Monkswell Tea House, and keeping this road until another road runs left-wards again, you turn up towards Chipstead. This is the easier route.

If you strike between the two paths, you can find another path that will land you well along this road. It is somewhat difficult to describe, as there are no landmarks to point the way, but the actual path is along a hedge about a quarter of a mile above the road. If you are too high up you will go wrong, and find yourself on a farm-track. So perhaps you had better take the road way, particularly if you desire to call at the tea-place.

Not quite half a mile along this road to Chipstead is a double cottage on the left, and a few yards beyond there is a footpath running towards a wood. This we take, and it is a very fine wooded way. At a junction of three paths, do not go over the stile in the corner, but keep to the middle path (forward). In about a mile and a half, watch for a path to your right, running by the edge of a field. At from twenty to thirty yards along this, a stile hidden round the corner shows the approach to a footpath to the road. If you go too far and miss this path, you will not find an exit free of barbed wire, and will have to retrace your way.

Proceeding along the field, keep left and come out at a stile in the corner. Turn rightwards to the viaduct, and if you need a tea-place Dene farm is only about a quarter of a mile along Chipstead Bottom. After tea, you can rejoin the route by taking a footpath opposite Dene farm and, turning right at the end, follow the road round to a main road, then right again to a pond, and turn leftwards. But leaving tea till Hooley is reached, take a road by the viaduct labelled 'Unsuitable for Motors,' and proceed along it till the pond at the main road is reached. Cross over the road, and go on with a pond on your left.

At the fork, keep left, passing Chipstead church on your right. This, in a short distance, brings us to Star Lane, Hooley, and ahead we see the top of Netherne hospital. The Hooley café is on the left, and 'buses run to Reigate (No. 414) and Redhill (Nos. 405 and 414).

To carry on, proceed along the lane opposite (to Netherne) passing over the railway, and when near the first gate a footpath on the left is followed. At the first field, go rightwards, coming out at a lane. Turn right again and, keeping forward past the cluster of houses belonging to Netherne hospital at the end, we find the remains of a stile and a path which runs by a wire fence and dips down. We are on the fringe of Farthing Downs.

At a fork, keep by this fence, going forward to an ascending path visible in the distance, and pass through an iron gateway. There is some fine country on both sides, and the path is very distinct, so this part of the walk is plain sailing. Coming by a copse on to a lane, do not go along the opposite woodland path which looks inviting, but turn right in the lane, which in a pleasant three-quarters of a mile brings us to Chaldon church.

Here I am going to ask even those people who do not usually enter any buildings of a religious character to change their mind and see this one. There are some mural paintings which will inform you of the various ways of 'going to hell.'

Go out towards the road you came by, and, less than a 100 yards beyond where you turned into the church road, look for two trees and the footpath which runs from them, past cottages, and on a road where, almost opposite, is an unmade road which goes in the same direction. At the end there is another footpath, still in the same direction, dropping down and coming up again. Soon after the rise do *not* go beyond the fence over a tiny bridge, but take the footpath continuing from a stile on the right. You will see hospital buildings well on your left (Caterham hospital). By keeping to this path, the road is reached where 'buses run back to Redhill *via* Merstham; or a left turn will take us, in about half a mile, to Caterham, where a 'bus can also be taken.

To continue, proceed by the road almost opposite (by a 'bus-shelter), and look for a notice on the right, 'Footpath to Hilltop.' Turn along here, and keep on until the path veers right, where, at the corner, there is a path over the fields. Then bear slightly left, by two black gates and towards a farm-house, where another stile leads to a road. On the other side of the road, there is a track. This, on entering the Downs (or Quarry Hangers),

KINGSWOOD

forks into three. Take the left one, uphill, and the first one downhill afterwards ; this winds round and finishes in Rockshaw Road.

A right turn along this road for half a mile will pass another path on the left, which drops down behind Merstham, coming into a road where the 'bus could be taken into Redhill. There is, however, a very nice footpath which may be used part of the way. Proceed under the railway-arch for the train or 'bus, but continue along the footpath if you are willing to walk right back to Redhill. The path enters a road and, turning right-wards at the first turning towards two railway-bridges, you take the road sign-posted to Nutfield, on the left.

There is a ruined church at a corner, where we turn along Battlebridge Lane and continue along Frenches Road till, just beyond the schools, we turn left-ward along Wiggie Lane.

This old lane runs into a path which goes by St. Annes and, just before reaching the small stream, you take a right path along its bank which will lead under the railway-station bridge. If, however, you are making for Reigate, continue past Nutfield Road (as given above) to the main road at Merstham, and go almost opposite through the entrance of Gatton Park and, after arriving near the house, turn left-wards by the lodge-gate at the finish of the long path, and then, by bearing right-wards, we get down to Reigate station.

While the whole distance has not been beyond fourteen miles, we have finished a good general round of the Reigate district, on the north side, and have travelled on many parts of the Pilgrim's Way.

IX. SOME SURREY FARMLANDS

Reigate Park, Reigate Heath, Buckland, Betchworth, River Mole, Dawes Green, Hales Bridge, Duxhurst, Landens, Salfords.

IF you are a stranger to Reigate, or are only familiar with its main thoroughfare, you are due for a surprise on this walk. From Reigate station, turn left, go towards the tunnel, and, after passing under it and going over the cross-roads, continue along Bell Street opposite. About 100 yards beyond Lesbourne Road, on the opposite side, is an entrance to Reigate Park. This is a wild, spacious park with great natural beauty—in fact, as fine a park as any in the south of England.

Take the broad, forward path running from the entrance, and keep on until another entrance is reached. Turn right here and, of two paths, take the uphill one ; on reaching the top, keep along the ridge past the seats for a good half-mile. On one side is Reigate Hill, with the water-tower prominent, and the Pilgrim's Way ; the other side will reveal the Weald below, and beyond that the hills which terminate in Leith Hill. A truly noble view for any park !

At the end of the ridge, by a clump of trees, take the left of two right-hand paths downhill, coming to an exit of the park, down some steps. Cross the road and go along the lane opposite (Sandy Lane). Keep to the lane, past some railings and by the side of a brook. Do not turn, however, through a gate (which may be open) labelled ' Private,' but continue where it becomes more of a footpath passing under a foot-bridge. Then go uphill to The Skimmington Castle (an inn) which you pass (unless you are anxious to stop), dropping on to the road on the left. In a few yards, look out on the left for the windmill (without sails) on Reigate Heath.

Cross over the golf-course to the path leading to the windmill (or rather to the right of it). Passing the entrance to the mill, which has been used as a church, continue along this path towards a house with the white rails of a small bridge showing in front of it. Keep along the path till it joins a narrow road. Here bear right-wards, past some silver-birch trees, and, when almost on the main road, a short-cut on the left leads to a house (Buckland Corner), at the right of which is our next footpath (just before a 'bus-stop).

This path lies back from the main road and may be missed if you are not observant, but it is separated from the house by a wire fence. Follow the path, and, on reaching a stile out of a field, follow the cart-track to the right. A short distance up this lane is The Jolly Farmer's inn, and there we meet the main Dorking road.

You may wonder why you have been brought back to a main road, but I am anxious to give you an opportunity to see Buckland church and its environment. The church is a quarter of a mile along the road, and opposite is a pond and tythe barn.

Go left, past the shops in Buckland, along the lane, and keep left. A sand-pit will be observed on the left—Buckland sand is well known, and large deposits are worked. The mill church can also be seen in the same direction. Look for a footpath by a cottage, and keep by the railings. Ignoring a well-worn path leading to some outbuildings, enter another field, where the railings are now on the right. At the end of the path, at a cross-path, turn left. With the gate at your back, either of the two paths ahead will lead to a wall, at the end of which a gate opens up a path through a lane, and half-right along an avenue of trees you will eventually arrive at a road, where you turn right-wards. Passing some delightful workmen's houses and a fine palatial home in the road, we are suddenly confronted by the river Mole—and the Dolphin inn.

Whether you call at the Dolphin Inn, look over the church, or admire the village street behind the church, depends on your time and inclinations. But turn left, away from the road you came by, and note the high path and facilities for releasing winter flood-waters.

Directly after crossing the bridge, note a path level with the river which is on the right-hand side of the bridge. This path is well marked, and goes uphill through wood and field, with peeps at the river and hills beyond. Eventually the path comes to a stile, but it is better to keep on to a second stile before joining the road.

Continue in the same direction towards the outskirts of Brockham Green, but do not attempt any footpaths which may be given on your map, as they can be extremely boggy. There is a curious farm-house, like a patchwork quilt, called Spiders Barn. Almost opposite a road, there is a gap into a field, by which a single tree acts as sentinel. This is our way. Keep left of the field, and go past a spinney into another field. A house is our objective and, as it may be muddy by direct approach, scout along the right of the ditch, where it may be jumped easily. Turn right along the lane, and cross over to a gate opposite. Boldly enter, as it is a public footpath, and keep to the left hedge. At the corner of the field the path continues into the adjoining field in the same direction ; over a tiny bridge and stile by a copse ; then diagonally over a field to a road (Dawes Green). Here turn right-wards for a few yards and along a road (sign-posted) to Newdigate.

There is a footpath over Westwood Common, but it is not recommended, as it is not only too swampy but difficult to trace. I have been down to my knees in mire during the winter. So it is better to put up with a bit of road and lane.

At the end of this road, continue along a road sign-posted to Newdigate. Half a mile beyond some white rails, between 'bus-stops on both sides of road, turn up a well-wooded lane. There are pleasant woodland paths here, secluded houses, and views through the trees of the Leith Hill range. In fact, it is a typical Surrey aspect until you suddenly come across a sign, ' Precision Engineers and Plastic Development.'

At a fork, bear left (before the plastic works), on to the main road, and cross over to the Charlwood road (sign-post). If you need it, the Surrey Oaks inn is only a few yards along to Newdigate. 'Buses go back to Redhill every two hours.

To continue the walk, keep to the Charlwood road, and fork left at the sign-post. This will bring you to a narrow bridge, Hales Bridge. The parapet of the bridge has been cracked, but the whole corner is worth pondering over.

Just beyond the farm, and on same side, there is an outhouse and telegraph-pole. On the left side of this, a gate opens up a path, passing over a gravelled entrance to a house. Pass along the side of a well-laid-out garden and house, and in a few yards the way lies through a small orchard (by gate), and not forward to the dark building ahead. Keep right, under the fir trees and over the ditch, then over a plank-bridge into a field, where you follow the cart-tracks left-wards. This track goes round the field, so, at the hedge, we turn right to a pond. Leave this on your left, and keep forward along the hedge to the end. At a gap in the trees, look for an open ditch or small stream. Follow this until a crossing-place is found. Climb the wooden rails, and in half a dozen yards on the right there is another gate, a typical keeper's gate. This leads to a copse, running just above and in the same direction as the small stream.

In springtime, it is usually full of wild

flowers, and is the earliest place locally for purple orchis. I have never been there in spring without finding something to reward me in the way of nature-study. Some of the rarer fungi have been obtained there, too.

It is as well to make sure of this path, as a mistake may take you well out of your way. It is backed by firs, which may be seen when coming up the field. The path veers left, past a dark forest of firs, and then by a large number of blackberry bushes which are loaded with fruit every year and seldom picked.

Get over a stile, keep along the left hedge, and climb over some iron rails. Turn sharp left, and climb over the first gate on your right. Then turn right to a stile, and make straight across the open field to a cattle-shed in ruins. On the right-hand side, there is a swing-gate. Go through this to a broken stile and a pond, where the farm of Chantisluer comes into view.

Ahead, cross the fields, and, on reaching the road, turn left to a house called Little Mynt. hurst, and then turn right. This farm-track runs along for a couple of miles, until Duxhurst farm is reached. Right, then first left by a pillar-box, then, instead of turning round by the lane, go forward to an iron gate on the right, and forward through a copse and field. Another gate then opens the way—rather overgrown—to the Brighton Road.

REIGATE HEATH

LODGE LANE

There is a tea-shop here, and there used to be a stile, but attempts have been made to stop the way, though it is marked on the map. If difficult to negotiate, the farm-track is a little lower down, and leads over the bridge, arriving at Landens farm and, later on, at Meath Green Lane. Left-wards, in about a mile, look for the entrance to Ladylands farm. A stile has lately been removed, but there is a right-of-way. Cross the field beyond and, in the top left-hand corner, there is a path leading to Lodge Lane. A right turn here will lead to the 'buses, trains and tea-places.

It is only a short 'bus-ride to Redhill, and you will have negotiated thirteen or fourteen miles of difficult country.

INDEX

INDEX—*continued*

INDEX—*continued*

Lightning Source UK Ltd.
Milton Keynes UK
UKOW030252161112

202254UK00001B/26/P